Escape from the
Taliban
August 2021

Fear, Fighting, Violence, and an Unclear Future!

By: Siam Pasarly

Edited by: Linda A. Keane

An Eyewitness Account of How the Taliban Retook Control of Afghanistan

Escape from the Taliban

August 16, 2021

Copyright © Siam Pasarly 10/28/2022

All Rights Reserved

No part of this book may be reproduced in any form, by photocopying or by any electronic or mechanical means, including information storage or retrieval systems, without permission in writing from the publisher.

The Return of the Taliban

Siam Pasarly

www.siampasarly.com

siamuden2009@gmail.com

+1 773.410.0092

Dedicated to

Giuliano Battiston and Robert Farrell

Contents

1.	The Taliban in 1994	7
2.	The USA Attacks the Taliban	11
3.	Growth and Success During War and Conflict	13
4.	"We Will Kill You, If…"	15
5.	Paying the Price for Democracy	17
6.	"You Should Leave Afghanistan!"	20
7.	I Should Go Back to Afghanistan	23
8.	August 15, 2021 - The Taliban Recaptures Afghanistan	26
9.	The Banks and ATMs Are Out of Money	28
10.	How Politicians Canceled my Airline Ticket?	30
11.	Sometimes Being Optimistic is Wrong	32
12.	Being Searched by the Taliban (Almost)	34
13.	"The Shameless Escape"	36
14.	Afghanistan Shuts Down	39
15.	Excellent News in a Horrible Situation	42
16.	Passing the Death Gate (Kabul International Airport)	45
17.	Five Nights of Sleeping on Stones and Dirt	51
18.	Departure to Bahrain	57
19.	Departure to Ethiopia	59
20.	Washington, D.C.	61
21.	Fort McCoy Army Base - Wisconsin, USA	64
22.	Treatment, Vaccinations, and Medical Checkups	70
23.	Dying is Easy; Getting Your Life Back is a Reward	73
24.	"Tarjoman Saib - Mr. Translator"	75
25.	The Joke That Came True	78
26.	Doing Good but Being Misunderstood	81
27.	Doing Business at Fort McCoy	86
28.	How I Fed My Family in Afghanistan from Fort McCoy	89
29.	My Family Should Leave India, But Where to Go?	92

30.	How I Resettled My Family in Pakistan	96
31.	My Daughter - "Hey, Baba, Send Us Tickets. Don't You Miss Me?"	100
32.	My Name Was Not on the List	103
33.	Love, Divorce, Rape, and Other Cases at the Base	106
34.	45 Days in "Prison."	109
35.	No Way to Pursue My Ph.D.	114
36.	Lack of Management Doesn't Mean We Have Bad Luck	116
37.	Emergency Conditions: "I Need to Get to Pakistan!"	119
38.	"Forget It! Peace in Afghanistan is Impossible!"	122
39.	My Wife's Operation in Pakistan	126
40.	God's Gift to Me	129
41.	The FBI and the DHS	134
42.	Conclusion	136

1. The Taliban in 1994

I was four years old when the Taliban first took control of Afghanistan. We were in Kabul, the capital of Afghanistan, and I recall it being a particularly hot summer. To escape the humidity trapped inside the house, we decided to sleep in the yard to get some outside air. We had no electricity inside the house for fans or coolers. As usual, when summer came, deep sleep disappeared like a cat to water. Full sleep was never possible due to the weather and constant mosquito bites. I would attempt to protect my body from the mosquitoes, but I had to choose between being covered and hot; or uncovered, cool but constantly tossing and turning to avoid the mosquitos. Sleep was also hard because I feared the scorpions that climbed the walls during the night.

Although it was difficult to sleep the first few hours of the night due to my fears, anxious thoughts, and physical tension; my body and mind eventually found the rest they needed around 3:30 a.m., when the weather became cooler, and the mosquitos disappeared.

One day, as I was enjoying my sleep and the cool weather outside, I was suddenly awakened by a huge blast! The earth shook; I was terrified and thought the explosion had occurred at our house. It was followed by many rounds of shooting. I began to cry as I saw bullets flying overhead. My father grabbed me and told me to go to the basement. But the basement was dark, and my fear of scorpions overwhelmed me. But my father didn't wait for a second; he ordered me to go.

Three years before the Taliban, another group, the Mujahideen, started capturing parts of Afghanistan and fighting each other. My father, who worked with the government, got the news that the Mujahideen had taken the Helmand province and were searching for houses to find those who worked with Russians and the Afghan government.

My father asked my mom to leave everything and immediately go to Kabul. We went to a relative's house. My father asked them to arrange a car with a reliable driver to move us to Kabul station. He made plans for his own safety by using a bus. We had nothing to eat or drink because in the rush, we left everything behind. We lived in a relative's house for a few days until my father made an arrangement with another homeowner to rent a room in their house in Kabul.

My grandmother often retold me the story of how we escaped the Mujahideen, I was too young to remember myself. I do remember asking her why the Mujahideen wanted to kill people who worked with the government. As I stood with my grandmother as she cooked, she would explain that the Mujahideen considered members of the government to be spies for Russia and not true Muslims because they fought with the Russians. Some of my best childhood memories are those with my grandmother, she showered me with love, cooked the most delicious food, and encouraged me to make a difference in the world. She said to me on several occasions, "My son, we have had terrible situations in Afghanistan, have lost countless people because of war and experienced poverty, illiteracy, poor governmental systems. I want you to be the president of Afghanistan. I want you to make positive changes in the country."

After the Mujahideen, the Taliban took over - those experiences are etched in my memory. The Taliban had strong control of key locations, stopped the Mujahideen civil war, but brought an extreme form of control took away many basic human rights, such as preventing women from going to school. and other groups from killing each other, and brought security. But there were serious problems as well. The women were not allowed to get an education or even go outside alone. The Taliban changed all the school subjects to Islamic studies, and those who knew Islam were the most respected people in society.

I wanted to be respected and important, so I started learning Islam. Besides reciting the holy Quran, I started to learn the Arabic translation. This is how I eventually learned Arabic. Every day I went to the Masjid, recited the holy Quran and gathered with Mulas. Watching TV, taking pictures, using the internet, and listening to music were banned and I grew up with those beliefs until 2001, when a new Afghan government was established and school curriculums changed again.

2. The USA Attacks the Taliban

A new war began in 2001, this time it lasted more than twenty years after the US attacked the Taliban. The Taliban lost their power, and the U.S. and other international community members supported and established a new temporary Afghan government. In 2004 we had an election, and Hamid Karzai became the president of Afghanistan.

The Afghan government with the help of the international community changed the schools' and universities' subjects and curriculums. School curriculum changed from being centered around Islamic studies, to include a more diversified array of subjects that included computer science and internet, English, and history lessons that touched on democracy, women's rights, human rights, and social change.

At twelve years old I worked in the flour market in order to support my family like my father.

My father worked as a Rickshaw driver (a type of small taxi). One day on a really hot day, around noon, while my father was driving the rickshaw, he spotted me carrying a 70 kg bag of flour (almost 155 pounds.) Watching me work so hard made him really sad, he stopped, hugged me, and helped me finish my work. Then he told me to go home and never go back to work. He said, "I am still alive, I am earning, and you don't need to work. You should just go to school."

Twenty years of war caused thousands of casualties. We lost family members, friends, and colleagues. The country endured not only the violence of war, but also poverty, starvation, lack of quality education and people lacked many basic humanitarian needs.

3. Growth and Success During War and Conflict

I grew up during years of conflict in Afghanistan. I became interested in political and social issues when I was a student. During my university years, I wrote articles on these subjects for magazines, newspapers, and online news channels which lead to my subsequent work with national and international organizations. I also wrote three books about the internet and children's rights.

We had been told many times that taking pictures and using the internet were illegal. However, my book *How to Use the Internet*, which was published by a well-known publishing house, Abdul Majid, in 2009, and

Afghanistan went viral. My second book about world-famous websites and information was published under the name *Web Pages* also did very well.

Although people were taught that using the internet was Haram (not lawful) in Islam, both books proved the demand for the internet was high and they exceeded people's expectations.

Though my family faced financial struggles and I had educational barriers as a child, I used the internet to learn more and then teach positive aspects of the internet and technology.

Slowly the media began to invite me for interviews and morning programs to have discussions about my books and social and political matters. Despite the challenges I was growing and succeeding well, until…

4. "We Will Kill You, If..."

I soon learned that working in the public eye had risks. For instance, I once had an interview on Radio Free Europe after the US military had killed Osama bin Laden, the founder of Al-Qaeda, a militant Islamist organization. I let it be known I was not in favor of the Taliban. One day at the office, while preparing to leave and meet one of my friends, I received a threatening phone call from a Taliban member warning me he knew where I lived, worked, and studied. "We have your complete information," he growled while threatening to kill me because I didn't understand how important Osama was to the Muslim world. In the background, I heard another person's voice saying to give me another chance. He agreed but warned me if it happened again, they would kill me.

I was shaken by the experience and how much they already knew about me. Their information about my home, university, and job was accurate. It was the first time I had been threatened, so as a precaution, I started limiting my interviews with the media for my safety and the safety of my family. This was hardly the vision I had for my country. My father advised me to avoid politics and focus on economic, social, and developmental issues. I took his advice.

I stopped traveling to the provinces where the Taliban were active during this time. Instead, I limited commuting to my office and work environment.

5. Paying the Price for Democracy

After graduating from the university, I was hired as a Communication and Marketing Expert with the Afghanistan Commercial Dispute Resolution Center in Kabul.

A year later, I joined the Afghanistan Chamber of Commerce and Investment as a PR Director and spokesperson. I began speaking to the public via different media on behalf of the private sector and the government. Then I joined the government as Senior Communication and Media Advisor. Gradually, I became an active member of the government.

Along with some of my friends, I wanted to be a change agent in Afghanistan. That choice was not without sacrifices. I lost some of my best friends in targeted killings, blasts, and kidnappings, friends who worked for freedom of speech, democracy, development, and human rights. The price for democracy was high.

The equality of women was also important to me. The development of a nation should be a shared responsibility between men and women. So I persuaded my wife to work for Afghan women. As a result, we formed an organization where we conducted national and international events, festivals, conferences, exhibitions, and Business to Business (B2B) meetings that included women.

Our big dream was to raise the standard of living and change the country's attitudes and ways of thinking. What we didn't anticipate was becoming a target for assassination. As we went about our activities, we received minor threats over the phone with warnings to abandon our activities. Usually, we ignored such messages and concentrated on our work. Then the threats became more serious and we had to limit our activities. Besides threats from insurgents, local government officials called, asking for a percentage of our earnings since some of our projects and events were funded by USAID, the UN, and other international organizations. We did our best to handle the work pressure, corrupt local officials, insurgents, and, later on, the Covid-19 Pandemic.

The threats and corruption took a toll on our sense of security. On October 12, 2020, we started to vary our schedules, changing the arrival and departure times from the office. After many horrible threats, I changed the location of our home to another one in Kabul. I loved to live in luxurious houses or apartments, but because of the security issues, I chose to live in simple places.

6. "You Should Leave Afghanistan!"

On a warm evening in February 2021, my wife and I began planning the International Women's Week Job and Education Fair. The weather was very nice in the morning, and it was beautiful outside. My wife was bored at home and wanted to visit the Kabul Serena Hotel to book it for our event. We went to the shop, bought things for my daughter, and then dropped her off at the Rasa Kindergarten. I was dressed casually and my wife told me that we had an official meeting and I should go home, change my clothes, shave my beard and look professional. So we went back home. It was around 10:00 am.

We left home. My wife was in the front seat drinking coffee while we were talking about the event design and format. While I was driving, a car exploded. We were very close to the explosions in Kabul's Dehmazang and Joy Sheer Street. I pushed the brakes hard and another car hit me from behind. I saw someone on fire and many casualties. Just a week earlier, I had witnessed another explosion very near where I was standing. My car was slightly damaged, but the threats became more frequent. We shared our concerns with the Deputy Minister of Interior and the police, but nothing changed. As a result, we canceled our event, stopped commuting and traveling, and closed our office. We had interviews with the BBC and Voice of America about these incidents that had made it necessary to close our office. (The videos are available online.)[1]

By March 2021, there didn't seem to be any way we could stay in Afghanistan. Friends who worked with the government called me and said, "You should leave

---

[1] Interview with VOA:

https://www.youtube.com/watch?v=uWLzipMg3CU&t=153s

Interview on direct threat to me with BBC

https://www.youtube.com/watch?v=CD9Xusw8wTU&t=47s

Afghanistan. At least for a while." So we moved to India, leaving everything behind: our business, home, office equipment, essential documents, and car, and moved to where we could feel safe. This decision was traumatic, and it caused my wife to have a miscarriage of our 8-month-old son.

7. I Should Go Back to Afghanistan

Because of all this trauma, I needed to keep busy, and do something I loved. I also needed something to do in India. So I decided to pursue a Ph.D. in Business Management and Digital Communication. It was going well. I wrote articles and published them as book chapters (How Do Entrepreneurship Ethics and CSR Affect Business Growth?) published in the Impact of Innovation & Entrepreneurship on Business Ecosystem. Digital Revolution and Entrepreneurship is another book chapter published.

In addition, one of my articles was published online via Academia Papers. (*How Digital Communication Accelerated and Internationalized the MSMEs During*

Covid-19). I enjoyed publishing and had outstanding scores at Sharda University, where I was pursuing my Ph.D.

Meanwhile, my wife wanted to begin English classes and admit our daughter to a school. She was also planning to start a business. Because I left Afghanistan in a hurry, I had a limited amount of money and we were short of cash. I needed to return to Afghanistan to withdraw money from the bank and check on my

business, my parents, and my brothers and sisters. Although the trip was necessary, I was excited about returning to Afghanistan and seeing my friends and family. I booked a ticket and left on August 13, 2021. Usually, I traveled with my wife and daughter, but this time, because the situation was not good, I traveled alone and reached Kabul late that night.

8. August 15, 2021 - The Taliban Recaptures Afghanistan

It was evening, and the weather was nice. I felt proud and had a smile on my face, because I was going to Kabul again. Kabul is my favorite city, a place where I have great memories. I called my friend, Mr. Abdullah Shuja and then went to his office. He explained the situation while we were drinking saffron tea and eating dried fruit. He emphasized that the Taliban might capture some provinces of Afghanistan, and were moving very strongly. He was also complaining about governmental corruption and weak leadership. Meanwhile, another friend called and said, "Look at the news! The Taliban has captured Mzaar–e Sharif, Herat, and Nangarhar provinces."

My tension doubled as I watched the news. It was around 10 p.m. My relatives had yet to hear I had returned to Afghanistan because I wanted to surprise them. Unfortunately, my surprise backfired. When I called a close relative, he was angry and started shouting, "What in the hell are you doing here?"

My relatives were shocked to learn I was back in Kabul. They told me not to go home or to the office, so I stayed in my friend Abdullah Shuja's office that night. Although the Taliban had captured the provincial offices, it was still hard to believe they would capture Kabul.

9. The Banks and ATMs Are Out of Money

The next day at 8:00 a.m., I booked a taxi but couldn't move even for a half-mile because of the traffic. I saw how people were moving and struggling to escape. Finally, I reached an ATM, only to find out it was down. It was 10:00 a.m., and there were thousands of people in front of the ATMs and banks attempting to withdraw money. The noise, traffic, and crowd affected me badly. I was looking at my contacts to see if I could find anyone to call and provide me with a VIP entrance. I called many bank workers, finally but reluctantly calling Mr. Omaid Salem, the CEO of Azizi Bank. When I called him, he told me they had no way of giving out any money because the central bank had banned all transactions. Then he asked me to wait while he managed the crowd, trying to get into the bank. I could see that he was under much pressure. At about the same time, my wife called and told me her family was in Kabul. They, too, needed money. She asked me to take her sister to the bank, but I explained that the banks were closed.

Almost six months earlier, before the Taliban took control, my family had been worried about my safety because of the direct threat from different insurgent groups. The situation in Afghanistan was horrible and beyond my control. I needed to leave. My family said I must go back to India. Meanwhile, I had heard that the Taliban was coming to Kabul from Nangarhar. So I changed the return date of my ticket from the next day to that day and went to the airport. When I entered the airport, I came to find a large crowd rushing to leave.

10. How Politicians Canceled my Airline Ticket?

It was 2:00 pm when I arrived at the airport. Everyone was struggling to leave Afghanistan, especially politicians, musicians, government officials, media analysts, and the general public. As I was crossing the crowd, I found many people knew me and expected me to help them pass the gate using my connections, but they didn't realize that I myself needed help. Finally, I reached the boarding area to check my ticket and collect my boarding pass. After long hours of waiting, the boarding pass was almost within my grasp when I was abruptly elbowed aside by some political leaders. They boarded the plane (with no apologies, I might add) while my ticket and those of others were abruptly canceled. Some officials had paid extraordinary amounts of money and used their influence to cancel our tickets. Meanwhile, my relatives called me again and again. When I explained the situation, I was advised to leave the airport as the Taliban had already reached Kabul. If they tried to enter the airport, there could be a high possibility of gunfire and shootings.

I am at the airport waiting for my boarding pass to leave for India

I left the airport and went to the apartment I had rented for my office. I asked a close relative if he had money. He, too, was running out of cash. I had only the taxi fare in my pocket.

11. Sometimes Being Optimistic is Wrong

Despite these incidents; I still thought the situation might improve. I wanted to be optimistic and planned a bank visit early the next day. I didn't know that the problem was about to worsen. Late that evening, I heard that President Ghani had left the country with his team. Even more alarming, the Taliban had entered Kabul. The situation was horrible. My heart was beating like a drum, not only for my own security but because of the dangerous condition. There was a high possibility of gunfire, explosions, and fights between the Taliban and the government. Since I was in Kabul, I uploaded a photo on Facebook showing I was in India busy with my studies. Then I changed my appearance in case I was sighted in the city. I didn't want anybody to think I was in Afghanistan.

About this time, my relative's friend called and told him the Taliban had started searching house-to-house for government officials and prominent people. I watched the color drain from my his face. He was having trouble speaking clearly. I tried to reassure him and boost his courage. He had asked his friends to come to the office for my protection. I told my relative to lock the door from the outside and then enter via the window, which he did. At midnight, the tower's main gate opened, and men armed with guns entered the building. They went to some apartments but fortunately passed ours.

12. Being Searched by the Taliban (Almost)

The situation seemed hopeless as I searched for ways to leave the city. I started sending e-mails to embassies, asking for their urgent support. I told my relative to leave to his family because they needed him. He didn't want to leave me alone, but I insisted. I knew I could handle the pressure and hide if needed. Finally, he left to his parent's house and I went to another relative's home. On the way, I saw the Taliban everywhere. When they stopped my car to ask questions, I tried to stay calm and answer them in a friendly manner.

The Taliban also wanted to search for my bag, which contained my laptop, passport, and other essential documents. I knew I could be arrested if the Taliban opened my computer. Quickly, I tried to divert his attention with a bit of flattery. "Hey, Mujahid, let me hug you and congratulate you on your victory. Let me take a picture of you." Once I had his attention, I continued, "You know, people are terrified of you. If you talk to them with a smile, they will relax and be friendly." With these few words, I was able to change the topic and divert his attention away from my bag.

After he had left, I went to a relative's house; they were shocked to see me and wondered how it was possible. "It was only yesterday you were in India," I said. "If you let me in, I will explain," I said, and I did.

These were days of uncertainty and fear for all Afghans. I was looking to find a way out of Kabul. On the other hand, my wife's family was also in Kabul and needed to settle somewhere they would feel safe. At the same time, I was texting and emailing my international friends, embassies, and the international community to help me find a way to get out of Afghanistan and get back to India.

13. "The Shameless Escape"

In lightning speed, the Taliban swept across the country, capturing the big provinces, including Kabul, within twenty-four hours, which was beyond the expectation of Afghans and the international community. The takeover of the Taliban was not easy for people to accept. Everyone was shocked and felt lost. The public's airline tickets were confiscated and reserved for the politicians, government officials, and Parliament members, who left the country as quickly as they could. Some fled to India, some to Pakistan, and others to Tajikistan and Iran.

After the Taliban took power, everything changed rapidly. Even before the Taliban had captured the Presidential Palace, more Afghan leaders fled: First Vice President Amrullah Saleh; Second Vice President

Sarwar Danish; Security Advisor Hamdullah Muhib, Afghanistan Administration Affairs Director Mahmood Fazly, some ministers, and the Afghanistan Bank Director. Their flight to unknown places became known as the "shameless escape." For everyday citizens, the absence of their leaders was frightening and made people despondent and even a little crazy. They had no choices except to hide or join the Taliban.

Even though the Afghan government had a trained Air Force and Special Forces, guns, vehicles, and access to advanced technology, they handed over everything to the Taliban. I saw an Army soldier begging to let him keep his gun. "There's no shame in having a gun," he begged. "If the enemy captures me, I'd rather fight than die." The commander ordered him to surrender his gun anyway.

I still have that scene in my mind, and it bothers me a lot. One of my friends who worked for the Afghan government told me the Taliban had gained access to the Afghan intelligence database with all its information. The Taliban was trying to find people who worked for the government in the rural areas where the Taliban was even stronger. My friend said these people were in great danger; some may already have been killed.

14. Afghanistan Shuts Down

We never ever expected these events nor did we have an idea of what would happen next. Things changed rapidly within twenty-four hours. Since the Taliban captured all of Afghanistan and the government officials escaped, everything closed down: the banking systems, factories, parks, commercial areas, and borders.

People with businesses, money in the bank, and projects to complete discovered that everything was gone. And it was even worse for those without money or resources. They didn't know where to turn for help.

Azizi bank is a private bank in Afghanistan; I took this picture on the first day the Taliban entered Kabul.

I contacted some young social and media activists who had spent half their lives promoting and advocating for social change and development. They were depressed and blamed President Ghani for the collapse of the government. They had three concerns. First, their ten to fifteen years of struggle, advocacy, and sacrifices had vanished; second, they feared a direct threat to them and their families; and third, their future was unclear. I prayed that no one should face such a dire future.

Afghanistan had turned into a non-functional country with closed borders. Flights were canceled, businesses and banks were closed, and government entities collapsed. People who had money in their accounts were begging for loans from others as they didn't have enough cash to buy food or feed their families. Everything was at a standstill: trade, production, services, and commuting. When the price of goods increased, no one had the cash to buy anything. Both the economic and social sides of life were severely affected.

Furthermore, well-known media channels and cable broadcasting went dead for twenty-four hours. As a result, there was no official news coming from Afghanistan. On the other hand, due to the un-digitalized facilities of the telecommunication companies, people abused the situation as a black market, selling scratch cards (credit cards) of (Afghan currency) 50 Afn for 100 Afn, effectively doubling the price.

15. Excellent News in a Horrible Situation

I tried different ways to leave the country and save my life. I called travel agencies for a flight out, which was impossible to obtain. The roads were also blocked. I had visas from Pakistan and India, which I could use for a flight, but all the national and international flights had been canceled. I thought about leaving by road to Pakistan and then to India, but my relatives told me the border was closed and to "Stay home or somewhere safe." They also advised me to ask someone to remove my billboards.

Recently, I had rented giant billboards in a prime location and had them printed with my image and the slogan "Be Your Own Boss." I had planned to organize a big event and promote it to have more clients.

I rented more than ten billboards to promote Be Your Own Boss Conference. This billboard was on the Kabul Jalalabad high way.

The company removed my banners except for the one on the main road to Kabul, which a friend removed.

Being a media analyst, social media influencer, and motivational speaker made my public life more difficult. Only those not in the public eye had peace of mind, while celebrities, media analysts, and government officials were constantly under the watchful eye of the Taliban.

This billboard was in front of Bagh-e-Zanana, Kabul, Afghanistan.

I had already shared my concern about the situation and emailed my network, the U.S. Embassy, the British Council, Canadian Embassy, the Italian Embassy, the German government, and Non-Governmental Organizations (NGOs). My best friend, Giuliano Battiston[2,] approached me on behalf of the Italian not-for-profit organization to say that he had put my name on the Italian evacuation list. It was excellent news. Later, the US Embassy team also sent me an airport pass and visa to enter the airport. It was the best news I had received yet. I relaxed… at least for a while.

---

[2] An Italian journalist who worked in Afghanistan

16. Passing the Death Gate (Kabul International Airport)

The US Embassy controls Hamid Karzai International airport, which was the only hope for Afghans, other nationalities, and international NGO employees to leave the country and fly to a safe zone. Thousands of people were struggling to enter the airport from different gates every day. On August 15, 2021, I went to the north gate, where thousands of people were crowded around the entrance. I was dismayed by the rush of people pushing and shoving to get into the airport and horrified by seeing dead or unconscious people cast aside. I was getting close to the gate when I saw two young girls, who looked to be 16 to 19 years old, lying on the ground with their private parts exposed. They appeared to be lifeless. I put my bag down and pulled them away from the crowd. When I splashed some water from my thermos on their faces, they began to show signs of life. I stepped away to retrieve my bag, but it had been stolen. When I looked back, the girls must have gotten up, as I could no longer see them in the crowd.

The airport had many gates, and thousands of people were at each entrance to the airport. I was in this gate.

My wife called and urged me to try getting into the airport the next day. Early in the morning, I was again on the way to the airport, but this time to meet my wife's family. Once more, I was stopped by the Taliban. In desperation, I told him my wife was pregnant and waiting for me to take her to the hospital. I pleaded with the Taliban to let me go, and he did. I breathed a sigh of relief, then called my sister-in-law, who was close to the airport door. I pushed through the crowd but lost my connection with my sister-in-law. I tried calling her repeatedly, but her phone wasn't working. Next, I called my mother-in-law to explain why we couldn't meet. She vented her anger and frustration because my phone wasn't working properly, and I didn't have enough credits to make more calls. Meanwhile, I called a relative and asked him to send me more mobile credits. By then, rumors were flying.

I heard seven young girls had died in the rush of people trying to get into the airport, and the bodies were sent to the Shino Zada Private Hospital. As I couldn't find my sisters-in-law, I worried about their lives and thought, "Could one of them be a relative?" I forgot about entering the airport and ran five to seven kilometers (three to four miles) to find a taxi to visit the hospital and check the bodies. Fortunately, my sisters-in-law were not among them.

After an hour of running here and there, my mother-in-law called to say they were waiting for us to go in together at the airport. Oh, my God, this was such good news! I returned for the third time to the airport, this time with my mother-in-law. Entering the airport had been a terrible experience, but the result was good. Still, rumors continued to circulate. I heard that the US was evacuating even those without passports. That explained why people from different provinces were trying to get into the airport. I also heard that the Taliban had been beating people. I saw more and more people pushing to get into the airport. To discourage them, the American soldiers used artificial gas and free fires to move back the crowd back.

The situation disappointed me because I could see how badly everyone wanted to leave our country.

Adults, kids, youths, and elders were pushing one another in their haste to enter the airport. People's faces looked drawn and desperate. Everyone was frightened. They didn't worry about their bags. Some women had expensive jewelry, but they left it behind because getting into the airport was more important.

At the same time, the Taliban was trying to stop people from leaving. I was beaten on the back with a gun, a Kalashnikov, and warned that they would shoot me in the head. They also punched me in the back. Still, I continued to try to get inside as I had my e-mail and entrance permission. After much gunfire and shouting, we were close to the airport gate, also known as *The Death Gate*. My sister-in-law was clever; she shared our details with a soldier at the airport who permitted us to go in. We were about to enter when an American marine pushed us back.

In frustration, I shouted, "Kill us or let us go inside. "Again, he pushed us back. All he cared about was managing the crowd. I tried another approach. "Put yourself in our shoes," I said in a calmer voice. I remember he was smiling, although I couldn't figure out why. It could have been the way I had mangled the English words. When my name was called again, "Pasarly, Pasarly," I saw someone, definitely not me, raise their hand. The soldier brought this impersonator and his family over to my sister-in-law and asked if they were her family. "No," she said firmly. "Please, don't send them away. Let them go inside." If it had not been for the kindness of my sister-in-law, they would have not been able to enter the airport. By letting these people go, we probably saved their lives.

17. Five Nights of Sleeping on Stones and Dirt

I was desperately thirsty when we finally got inside the airport and gladly accepted some water from an American marine. After the security scan, we went to an area where people were waiting for the buses.

Struggling to pass the airport gate

Nearly two thousand people were there by 10:00 p.m. We waited a long time, but the buses didn't come because of the crowd.

My family was worried about me. I kept them informed from time to time until my phone was about to die. Quickly, I called my relatives to explain the situation and assure them I was safe inside the airport. I told them I would only turn on my phone if anything urgent happened. I asked my relatives to call my wife and let her that her family was safe.[3] By then, it was midnight, and I had fallen asleep on the stone and dirty food packets. At 3:00 a.m., the soldiers came and asked us to follow them. It was dark, and we couldn't see the road ahead. On the other hand, because of the crowd and dust, it was difficult to recognize the faces. There was also a rumor that they were taking us outside. My sisters-in-law and I stopped to evaluate the situation, but we had no other option but to follow the soldiers.

My younger sisters-in-law could walk fast, but my brother-in-law and mother-in-law had health problems, and I helped them walk. After a while, the soldiers stopped and told us to stay in line. They were letting

---

[3] My wife and daughter were in India.

thirty people at a time board the buses. Finally, we reached an enclosed area inside the airport. Again I called my relatives and explained that I was okay and safe. I was asked the question we all wanted to know. *Where are you going?* At 7:00 a.m., the American soldiers brought us a breakfast of ready-made food and water. Almost none of us could eat the food because it was not what we were used to; it tasted

These pictures are from inside the airport

different, and we didn't know if it had pork, which we could not eat. People picked and ate the food they recognized and left the food that was unfamiliar.

After a day, disappointing news spread that American soldiers would pick us up and take us back to Kandahar Province. Luckily, the rumor was false. The marine explained that because the Taliban had seen us entering the airport, there was a possibility that we could be arrested if we went outside. He said if anyone wants to go home, they should go through the proper channels. By this time, the weather was getting colder, and almost none of us had warm clothing. I came up with an idea of how to keep warm. The meal the soldiers gave us had carbon in the plastic used to warm the food. I suggested putting water in the plastic as it would stay hot for one to two hours and we could use it to sleep. I learned this from my father, who was a chemistry teacher.

We had no electricity to charge our phones; I used my laptop to charge my phone. To maintain a longer charge, I kept the brightness of my phone and laptop at zero. Some of my relatives also wanted to enter the airport, but they were stopped. To be honest, it was not clear where we were going. Between the hot

Picture from the airport

sun during the day and no heat at night, we could not sleep very well.

No one had peace of mind. I saw pain, sorrow, and tension in all of us. Another rumor that caused distress was that the Americans were checking documents and only allowing those with American passports or green cards to leave. At first, we believed the rumors were true because the soldiers were coming and asking for Canadian or American passport holders. We were baffled. Everyone was trying to show their documents and explaining: "I have the SIV case, I have the airport visa pass, I worked for the US embassy or USAID."

Fortunately, I had another option. I could join the Italian evacuation if the Americans didn't evacuate me. I had already put my name on their list. This unclear status made people anxious. Everyone was trying to talk to the marines or their commanders to get the correct information. Unfortunately, no one was sharing information. I hid my tears of disappointment at this lack of helpfulness.

After five terrible nights at the airport, it took another night to reach the airplane, just three to four km away (less than two-and-a-half miles).

At last, we boarded the aircraft!

It had been challenging for the marines to manage the crowd and also take care of the airport, which was under the watchful eye of the Taliban. *(It is not easy to write this story. I am reminded of that fear and anxiety as I write.)*

18. Departure to Bahrain

Once on the aircraft, we still didn't know our destination. Around 500 people sat cross-legged on the floor of the plane, all cramped together for five hours. After landing, I looked outside and saw a sign, "Welcome to Bahrain" and other Arabic words. It was the second time I had visited Bahrain. It is a beautiful country. I had a great time on my first visit. I told my sisters-in-law and other friends about Bahrain.

We then boarded a bus. I looked forward to seeing the base as I had never been to a military base. Every family was guided to different rooms. We were shown a room that was large enough for all five of us. After relaxing for a while, we went to dinner. I have traveled a lot and tried different foods, but this meal was delicious, although I might have been influenced by not having had a proper meal for eight days. After dinner, we were provided toiletries and sandals. Everyone made a bee-line to the showers as we hadn't changed our clothes for almost ten days. In the morning, the soldiers came and asked us to board the buses—destination unknown.

Inside an aircraft leaving Afghanistan – photo by Reuters

19. Departure to Ethiopia

After being briefed in the security area, we were taken to an Ethiopian airplane. We were disappointed because we had expected to go to the U.S. Nevertheless, I took pictures of the aircraft and shared them via WhatsApp with my Ethiopian Ph.D. classmate in India. We had a good time. I shared information about Bahrain and Ethiopia with my family. During the flight, I checked the destination and saw that we were not going to Ethiopia. We were on our way to Washington, D.C. I was thrilled with the change in plans and shared the new destination with my family.

Airplane photo - departure from Bahrain US military base

20. Washington, D.C.

Washington, D.C., the capital of the United States, is a famous city I have heard much about through the media. We finally landed in this historic and beautiful city. At the airport, I noticed the happiness on the faces of every Afghan. They were laughing and talking, which made me feel much better. I was searching for a way to call my friends in Washington. After the security check and reviewing our documents, they gave us different hand-built tags and invited us for lunch. After we used the airport showers, the soldiers put us on buses. We thought they were taking us to a specific area and that we would then be able to go by taxi into the city.

As I was translating for the Afghans, everyone on the plane was asking me, "Where are we going?" I, too, wanted to know. I called my friend and relative, Selab Sulaimankhel, to ask if he would pick some of us up at the Washington airport gate. In the meantime, I noticed our bus was not taking us outside the airport but had stopped next to another airplane. Quickly, I called my friend in Washington and told him not to come. We waited at the aircraft for a while until everyone had arrived. I've had many experiences traveling by air, and the pilots or flight attendants always give out

A picture taken from the public domain shows Afghan refugees arriving in Washington, D.C.

Information about your destination and the flight duration. This flight was quite different. No one gave us any information. After a two-hour flight, we landed at Fort McCoy in Wisconsin. Surprise!

21. Fort McCoy Army Base - Wisconsin, USA

Arrived in Wisconsin, Fort McCoy Military base

After the airplane landed at Fort McCoy, the buses arrived. An Army officer explained the rules and regulations. "This is a military base, and you will be limited to your barracks," he said. "If you hear gunfire or explosions, don't worry. Fort McCoy is a military training area." We were also warned not to go into the forest where wild animals might hurt us. Finally, we were taken to Barrack 2517. We were each assigned a bed and a box to keep our belongings. The Red Cross provided us with blankets and toiletry items.

The bigger problem was the toilets, which had walls but were not completely enclosed. I spoke English, so I shared this problem with the Army. It was decided the men would use the upstairs toilets and the women the downstairs toilets. After that, the Army asked me to help them translate to other buildings.

I interpreted from English to Pashto and Dari Languages.
Asylum orientation workshop, Fort McCoy Military base

I acquired the name *Tarjoman Sahib - Mr. Translator*. More on this later. As we had not eaten much in the last few days, the Army directed us to the "grab-and-go" food and beverage area. It was self-service, so you could take as much as you wanted. The "guests" took much more. I explained that they were to take only as much as they needed, but no one listened. In addition, the Army was unprepared for feeding so many so quickly. Eventually, they provided only fruits and beverages. It was a big headache for the soldiers and food distributors.

After a day, we noticed the lack of privacy in our sleeping area without walls. Sleeping so close to one another was uncomfortable, so we asked the soldiers to provide curtains to separate the beds. The Red Cross and volunteers were very supportive, thanks to them. They provided us with blankets, curtains, and other facilities for the sleeping areas. Still, we looked forward to leaving in the next few days.

The Barak, where we lived temporarily

Additional special thanks go to those who donated their equipment, entertainment, and tools and bought new materials for our kids at the military base. Some Afghans started free English language classes. Later on, another organization continued these classes. The Chamber of Commerce provided job training. They developed an online platform called "Hire Our Heroes." Other organizations opened their branches to support us by writing resumes and teaching us how to apply for jobs. From the beginning until the end, we had outstanding laundry facilities. We brought in our clothes, and they were washed within a day. Good people worked there. They were very friendly and always had smiles on their faces.

Still, there were over 15,000 refugees who now lived at this base. Although food, beverages, fruits, and clothing were provided, everyone still had the same question: *When are we going to leave?* No one had the answer.

We often stood in long lines for food.

22. Treatment, Vaccinations, and Medical Checkups

If you want to enter the United States of America, you need to complete your medical checkup and have your report in your hand. Almost all of us evacuated to US military bases had not been vaccinated. The US Public Health Department initiated vaccinations and medical checkups. We thought that after the medical checkup, they would resettle us outside the base. Instead, the Public Health Department started Covid-19 vaccinations. We had a good experience with the first vaccination, with only a few aches, despite fears of injections and negative attitudes about vaccinations in general. After we had completed the first vaccination, we were told the next one would be in twenty-one days.

The medical clinic facilities could have been better in the beginning. We raised the issue in our weekly meeting with representatives from the State Department, IRC, IOM, the Chief Commander, and representatives from the barracks. Fortunately, these people were receptive to our needs and good at making decisions. As a result, they changed the health clinic team and expanded their branches to many locations inside the military base, which helped reduce the wait time for treatments.

The medical doctors were very friendly and welcomed us. They learned some Pashto and Dari words and used them whenever they interacted with us. For instance, my brother-in-law had been in pain since he left Afghanistan. When we reached the base, he complained many times. I took him to the clinic but was told they only accepted emergency cases. For other complaints and treatments, we were advised to get treatment outside as they had limited resources. At first, I didn't take my brother-in-law's sickness seriously as he tended to be a chronic complainer. But his condition worsened and we called an ambulance.

At the clinic, the medical doctor told us they only accepted emergency cases. To us, his condition was an emergency. Finally, the doctor prescribed some tablets. After a few days, my brother-in-law had finished his medicine. While searching the label for a refill, he discovered his medication was expired. I checked the label, and sure enough, my brother-in-law was right. He was lucky not to have had a negative reaction. We returned to the clinic, and I asked the MD about the expiration date on the bottle. "I believe this is the manufacturing date," he said. "If so, you must have gotten the medication very fast, as this is the same date we visited your clinic," I said. The doctor confirmed that the date on the bottle was the date he had given us the medicine. On the other hand, I saw people who were not seriously ill go to the clinic anyway. "If you're OK, why do you keep coming here?" I asked one man. In a whisper, he replied, "If they see you are sick, they will resettle you more quickly to the city." People who were sick and old and families with kids were given priority.

23. Dying is Easy; Getting Your Life Back is a Reward

After the first vaccination, we waited another twenty-one days before the medical staff called us for the second shot, which was quite strong. It was around 10:00 a.m. when we went to the clinic, and they gave injections to my sister-in-law. I encouraged them to stay calm and take it easy. However, I didn't know that my own condition was about to worsen. When the medical staff prepared to inject me, I was all right initially, but then an inexperienced nurse lost my vein repeatedly. He tried another vein but couldn't find that one either. With blood collecting under my hand's skin, I felt woozy. I asked the nurse to stop for a while because I was not feeling well. "Be strong," he said and continued searching for a vein, this time in my other hand. That's when I fainted. I didn't regain consciousness for *five minutes* until someone slapped my face. When I woke up and opened my eyes, I was surrounded by the medical staff, my mother-in-law, and others. The chief doctor reassured me that everything was all right and to relax. They started checking my blood pressure and gave me sweets to eat. I was carried to another room and told to lie down for a while. After a few minutes, a doctor came in. "Thank God you're back," She said. "We even called an ambulance."

Dying is not difficult. Getting my life back and writing this book for my beloved readers are the rewards. They say people who have an easy death are lucky. Actually, the luckiest people are those who return to the living world.

24. "Tarjoman Saib - Mr. Translator"

I love working with people and enjoy helping them. As I had a good command of English, everyone expected me to translate for them. In the beginning, there was a limited need for Afghan translators. As requests increased, the State Department hired many Afghan translators. I was asked to translate for the Army's office staff. I was *Tajorman Saib, Mr. Translator*. In that role, I attended meetings in various departments and provided translations. On behalf of the guests, I negotiated with the Army and the kitchen owner regarding food and facilities. Then I delivered the exact information to the guests, going from building to building. Meanwhile, everyone was asking two questions. First, when are we leaving the camp? Second, how can we evacuate our families from

Afghanistan? I asked various offices these questions - the marines, State Department, IOM, Legal Office, and IRC. No one had a definite answer. I often asked the State Department staff and was told they didn't know the answers either. Then I asked if they could at least tell us when we were leaving. The best answer I got was it would be a matter of weeks, not days. As for me, I was told I would be transferred once my medical checkup, documentation, and resettlement issues were completed.

Helping others was often a challenge. Some people asked questions, and I knew the answers, but they didn't trust me and insisted on "official" answers. When I asked the appropriate staff, I was told they had already answered these questions many times, and since I knew the answers, I should be the one to answer them. Others thought because I knew English, I was getting more clothes and food, which wasn't true.

We had all kinds of people on the base - literate and illiterate, good and bad, industrious and lazy, and more. It was challenging to manage such a varied assortment of people. In the beginning, my sister-in-law Mrs. Raihana Noorzai and I had a lot of energy and enjoyed volunteering. She was translating and supporting female guests while I was helping the male guests. I salute the Army's tolerance. They were very kind and helpful.

25. The Joke That Came True

From leaving Afghanistan to my arrival at the Fort McCoy military base, I was helping fellow Afghans with translation and easing their adjustment to a new environment. At Fort McCoy, that meant helping Afghan refugees follow the military's protocol and discipline. We changed the menu many times as we couldn't always eat the food served on the base. To keep Afghans occupied and informed, I wrote information on small banners in Pashto and Dari, the Afghan languages, so they could understand resettlement issues, the evacuation process, and daily activities.

Shortly after that, my responsibilities were expanded to include maintenance of the base, which meant training people on various cleaning systems. It was an exhausting job, as my people often came to me late at night with requests for translation or to advise them on personal problems. I was also listening to hundreds of stories from the Afghans regarding their families left in Afghanistan. I was translating for the legal department lawyers, volunteer attorneys, and the State Department. I created a WhatsApp group named Afghan Network in America. Through this group, we were communicating issues of importance to each other. After two months, people were asking me why I was still there. They thought because I spoke English and my financial situation was secure, I would have left by then. They were unaware of my problems and I often joked that I would be the last person to leave. "I am your representative, so I will leave after all of you have left." That joke turned out to be true, as I was in the last group of Afghans to leave the base.

There were many kitchens on the base. Both men and women managed the food lines in their own areas, which meant I was only responsible for my area. In the beginning, there were always problems with food distribution. People stood in line early in the morning to ensure they got enough food. Almost every day, some people tried to jump ahead in the line, which created conflicts between guests. It was hard to manage, but fortunately, people appreciated me for managing the lines…usually.

26. Doing Good but Being Misunderstood

Most refugees left Afghanistan with basic possessions: one set of clothing and no cash. We needed everything: shirts, sweaters, jackets, and trousers. Initially, the Red Cross distributed clothing, but it was very uneven. Some people got twice as much as they needed, while others stood in long lines in front of the Red Cross office and received only one outfit. The Red Cross soldiers were a great help in managing this situation. They separated the clothing and other basic needs for distribution. Still, we spent lots of time standing in lines. Everyone was happy when they finally received some clothes as no one had more than one outfit. For instance, I had left Afghanistan with only one set of clothes and my laptop. I spent twenty-five or thirty days wearing the same shirt and pants. When I went to buy some clothes with my MasterCard, I discovered the Taliban had blocked my card. No matter how wealthy or successful people were back home, in this new country everyone was starting over again.

I helped organize the line, reading names and stopping to chat with each person. Some people thought I was doing this to be first in line and get the best clothing. Even one or two people from my own building thought I was trying to take advantage of the situation. To be honest, it had nothing to do with clothes. I was trying to support the people who had to stand in line for such a

Afghan Refugees are waiting for food. I was usually managing the line.

long time. It never occurred to me that someone would think I was taking advantage of the situation. When I looked at it from their point of view, I could see my actions had been misunderstood.

Life has ups and downs. I try to take it easy and ride the waves. There are different types of people: good and bad, and those who value your efforts and those who don't. I believe it's important always to do the right thing, no matter what people think. This is my mindset and the way I live my life. After realizing what some people thought, I took my place at the end of the line and stopped offering my support, at least while standing in line, as it obviously had been misunderstood.

Many volunteers supported us through difficult times and brought smiles to our faces. We are thankful to all those who came in their cars loaded with clothing and food, as well as bicycles, balls, and games for kids. Other people contributed money. Their kindness was really touching, I did not expect that people will show up to the military bases to check on us and bring us what we needed. We will be ever grateful to all the people who have supported us, earning our love and gratitude for their generosity.

I met the retired ambassador, Mr. Greg Schulte, at the Red Cross office. He was such a nice person. I took down his contact information and shared it with others. He introduced us to his wife, Nancy, and friend Elizabeth Blair. Ms. Blair also supported Afghan refugees. She asked us to send clothing sizes and a list of any other items we needed urgently. After a few days, I received a notice to pick up these items, only to discover that they would take another two days to reach me because they were coming from a military area. When my sister-in-law and I received the items, we were so excited to finally receive them that we opened the package in front of the post office. We had thought they would be used, but everything was new: clothing, a bread-making machine, and other items. Generosity is not limited by geographical borders, race, or religion.

"Thank you very much, Mr. Greg and Elizabeth Blair. It's been a long time since I have seen my sisters-in-law this happy. You brought smiles to their faces." My sister-in-law Raihana also texted Elizabeth Blair and thanked her for her support. I also decided to always support refugees as I understand how difficult it is to leave your country and be separated from your wife, children, father, and mother.

Mr. Greg and Elizabeth Blair sent me these gifts

27. Doing Business at Fort McCoy

After leaving Afghanistan with my equipment and belongings, only 150 euros were left from what I had borrowed from one of my relatives.

When I reached Fort McCoy, I went to the PX store to shop. I offered euros, but PX didn't accept other currencies. Even when I offered to change my euros very cheaply, I was told they had only limited services and couldn't accommodate me.

I drank energy drinks when I worked, especially while writing my books or studying. I don't recommend energy drinks because of their long-term side effects. My sister-in-law had only USD 20. We spent $10 on energy drinks and kept the remaining $10 for another time. Unfortunately, my sister-in-law lost the remaining $10.

I was good at filing Special Immigration Visas (SIV) applications and case management, writing letters, biographies, emails, and resumes. In the beginning, I volunteered to provide these services. When people heard it was free, they came at all times of the day and late at night. I began losing sleep and had trouble focusing on other tasks. We decided to charge very low monetary fees to make the service more manageable. It was a great decision as it limited the number of people to those really in need of the service. However, it didn't solve the problem for those with no money. We were sympathetic to their situation as they had left Afghanistan with little more than the clothes on their backs. We decided to provide free help as long as they didn't tell anyone. We also offered other services to

raise money. I am very good at repairing Microsoft Windows and installing other computer software. Other people with skills, like barbers, offered their services, so we could earn a few dollars and buy energy drinks.

I earned this amount of money from those who had money. For people who didn't have money, I volunteered my services.

28. How I Fed My Family in Afghanistan from Fort McCoy

When the Taliban swept across Afghanistan and took control of its government, it created a financial impact on Afghans. For instance, the Azizi Bank blocked my MasterCard, and I could not withdraw or send money via Money Gram or Western Union. The financial situation of my family in Afghanistan was also bad. Although my father was working as a lecturer at the university, he had not received his salary for months. I made a few videos for YouTube and designed promotional banners. On Facebook, I posted my services: writing resumes and contracts. A day later, I got requests from Afghanistan to do these small projects. When the projects were finished, I asked the recipients to send the money to my father's account. My brothers began promoting this service to attract more clients. These efforts became a way of paying my family's basic expenses.

On November 21, my friend Mr. Giuliano Battiston, who had helped me get out of Afghanistan, went to Jalalabad and visited my father. Before he left for Afghanistan, he asked if my family needed money or financial support. I politely said we were in need but didn't want to bother him. He was clever at reading between the lines and understood my situation. After that, he gave money to my father. There is a saying that good friends are God-gifted. My friend was such a man: God gifted him with a beautiful heart. He helped me through one of my worst times. His generosity meant a lot to me.

I also learned a valuable lesson: Never give up. God will meet you at the level of your efforts. If you struggle, God will support you with more rewards. It has been my experience that God loves hard-working people. God never, ever failed me in any job that I have had. I am proud of all my friends, especially those who helped me through one of my most difficult times, like Mr. Battiston. *Grazie mio, miglior amico.* [4]

---

[4] Thank you, my best friend

29. My Family Should Leave India, But Where to Go?

As mentioned, on August 13, 2021, I left Afghanistan to go to India, where my wife and five-year-old daughter lived. After emigrating to the United States, I searched for any way to invite them here. I knocked on many doors, searched online and offline, called friends, and e-mailed the embassies, responsible organizations, and humanitarian associations. There seemed to be no way to evacuate them. Life in India was no longer good for my wife because she was pregnant. Nor was life good for our daughter because she couldn't attend school.

Meanwhile, we had heard that the US Embassy was starting the evacuation procedure from Afghanistan. Thus, we decided that my wife and our daughter should leave India for Pakistan because it would make it easier for her to leave to the U.S. Getting a Pakistan visa was another headache. I called my friends and travel agencies in Afghanistan to book an online visa. The visa price and travel agency commission were high as everyone wanted to leave Afghanistan. After fifteen days, I was able to get visas for my family. Next, we faced ticket problems. There are no direct flights between India and Pakistan because these two countries are in conflict. So I needed to book tickets to Sharjah (a city in the United Arab Emirates) and then to Pakistan.

These were the days when we counted every cent because we had no access to our bank accounts or Mastercard. We were running out of money to pay for the flight tickets. When I was in India, I bought video production equipment such as an HD camera, Mac 4k PC, lights, and stands for my YouTube channel. I asked my wife to sell this equipment. I also uploaded photographs on online sales platforms to sell them quickly. My wife found a few people to buy the equipment but at a very low price. We sold almost everything at a 60 percent discount. I rented an apartment in India for six months with a two-month advance as a security deposit. When we were getting ready to leave, I asked my wife to collect the money for the advance from the apartment owner. I have good memories of India and especially the people. The apartment owner was the exception. He did not want to refund the advance money to my wife, especially after he found out I was no longer in India. This created a problem for us as we were on a tight budget. I called the property dealer and broker, who was our middleman, to solve this problem. After one or two days of conflict and negotiation, the dealer returned the advance money to my wife. My wife moved from the greater Noida part of India to New Delhi, where other Afghans live. They stayed there for a few days and then departed for Sharjah International Airport. Unfortunately, they left India with bad memories.

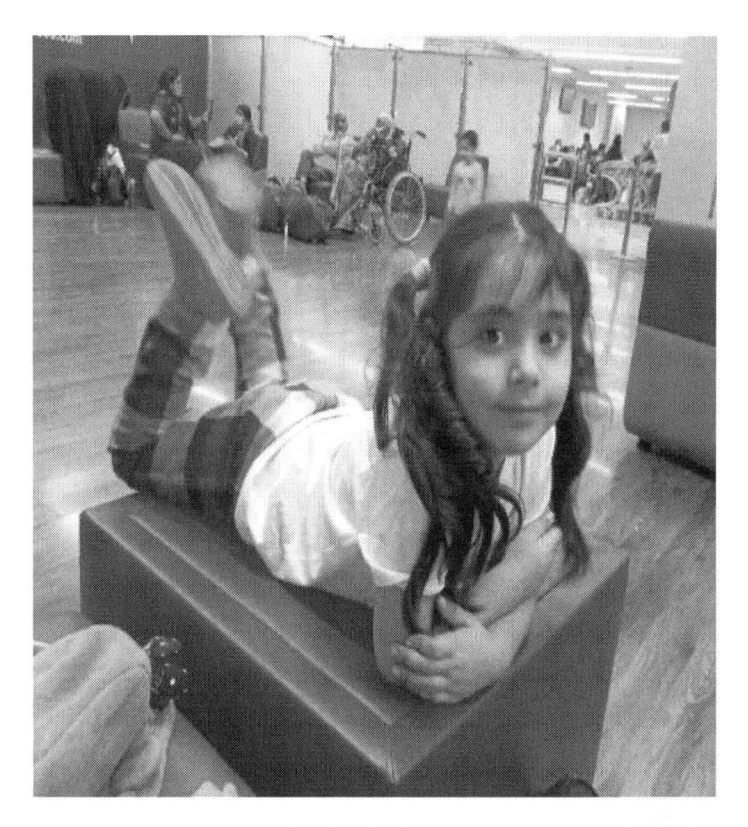

My daughter is waiting for her flight to Pakistan at the Sharjah International Airport.

30. How I Resettled My Family in Pakistan

After a two-hour flight, they landed at Sharjah International Airport in the United Arab Emirates. As their flight was to Peshawar in Pakistan, they waited in the airport terminal for ten to twelve hours. My wife completed the paperwork and went through a rigorous security checkup because she had came from India and was going to Pakistan. The Pakistani officials asked many questions. When my wife and daughter were about to board the airplane, the boarding manager asked them to produce their Covid-19 vaccination document. Although my wife had received the Covid vaccination, she did not have the proof. Thus, she wasn't allowed to depart until she provided verification. After many negotiations with the boarding manager and other officials, their papers were rejected, and she was told they would be sent back to India. As my wife was pregnant, there was no specific place for her to sleep and rest. Unfortunately, the news that she would be sent back to India was very upsetting to her.

Meanwhile, I was in communication with the airport boarding workers in Pakistan while she struggled to solve the problem herself. Finally, my wife made an official complaint in which she wrote that if proof of a Covid vaccination was required, why had she not been informed of it before she departed from India? The Complaint office collected the information and documents and shared them with their headquarters. After seven or eight hours of negotiations and a struggle to solve the problem via e-mail and phone calls, the airline officials said they were sorry but unconvinced. They booked a room in a hotel for my wife and daughter and rescheduled them for an upcoming flight. After nearly sixteen hours of waiting, they finally flew to Peshawar. The real issue preventing my family from flying wasn't a lack of documentation but the problems between India and Pakistan.

Since I had not slept during these negotiations, which were ongoing at night in the US, I finally took a nap.

I was thankful that we had not given up, even though it had been difficult to handle my family's flight arrangements from afar and see them safely on their way to Pakistan.

When they reached Peshawar, I had already asked my good friend and Afghan national businessman, Mr. Baz Muhammad Afsarzai, to send his driver to pick up my family from the airport and bring them to his house. Our families used to socialize when we lived in Afghanistan. Good friends are gifts from God. Mr. Baz Mohammad Afsarzai and Mr. Haji Enayat Afsarzai are very kind people with great families. They were very supportive of my wife. Without them, my family might have found it more challenging to resettle in an unfamiliar city. God bless them.

After a day's sleep, I started searching and screening houses and apartments online. I also called my friends in Peshawar to assist my wife in finding an apartment. Many Afghans have emigrated to Pakistan because of the Taliban, so good houses and apartments were difficult to find. Finally, we found an apartment in

Peshawar after several days of searching. I wrote a comprehensive biography for my wife and started sending it to the embassies and UNHCR (United Nations High Commission for Refugees) office for registration. However, cases took longer than usual to register with UNHCR; we would be fortunate to have it done within a month. I asked my wife not to consider moving again while she was pregnant. I promised that if she took care of herself and our daughter, I would handle the stress of finding ways to evacuate her and our daughter to the United States.

31. My Daughter - "Hey, Baba, Send Us Tickets. Don't You Miss Me?"

It was impossible for me to stop my tears when my five-year-old daughter Malala Pasarly called me. She was crying, "Baba, you don't miss me? I asked you many times to send me a plane ticket. I want to come to you or you to come here." I was not feeling well after I listened to her words of love for me. I just turned off the camera so she would not see my tears. After a few minutes, I told her that I was trying to find airline tickets for her. "Don't worry, Baba will find tickets for you." She said I was telling her a lie. "Search your laptop now; you can find more tickets." She thought that airline tickets were issued from laptops because that is the way she had seen travel agents produce tickets. I told her, "Ok, give me some time, and I will send you the ticket but there is no airplane to evacuate you right now. "Ok," she said. "I will come by car." I told her that wasn't possible either. She had to come by air. A day later, she called again. "Baba, why are you telling me lies? I saw an airplane from our apartment last night." I was not able to talk or answer anymore. She was right. I did lie to her because I didn't think she would understand the situation. The next best thing I could do was send a ticket to Pakistan and resettle our family there.

Almost three months passed, and my daughter continued asking for a ticket to wherever I was living. I made grand promises, telling her that she was the luckiest girl in the world. I would provide her with the best education at the best school. When we were in Afghanistan, my daughter could meet Ashraf Ghani, our President, and Mr. Hamid Karzai, the ex-president, and Parliament members, and attend major events such as Independence Day, cultural conferences, and exhibitions. Every morning, I left her at the nursery and picked her up in the evening. I played with her, told jokes, and took her shopping. Sometimes she went to the university with me while teaching in Afghanistan. She is a clever kid, and I hope I can find a way to give her the good life we had in Afghanistan. She can go far in the world if I provide suitable facilities and work with her; she has already demonstrated her intelligence, thoughtfulness, and creativity.

Being separated from my family was difficult, some in Afghanistan and others in Pakistan. When I was with my in-laws at Fort McCoy, I was responsible for supporting them as well as doing my job at the base. It wasn't easy to handle a multitude of responsibilities. After my in-laws left the military base, I relaxed as they settled, and my daily responsibilities became more manageable.

32. My Name Was Not on the List

I was attending the weekly meetings when I made a request to facilitate and expedite our resettlement process. The IRC and IOM said this was not in their area of responsibility. As soon as the resettlement agency had picked my case, they would facilitate my departure. They persuaded us that if we were to leave the base on our own, we would not have benefits that included a rental house for three months and an application for a work permit. As I was new and had left all my belongings in Afghanistan, I had no other option but to wait. Meanwhile, one of my friends, Gul Sayar, told me if I applied to a resettlement agency, they would pick my case, which is what he had done. I started e-mailing various agencies. Refugee One from Chicago answered my e-mail and asked for more detailed information. I sent the required information but was told I should submit my case to the International Organization for Migration (IOM). The communication took almost a month with no results. I referred to Sima Quraishi, the director of the Muslim Women Resource Center in Chicago, and shared my information with her. It was late at night, around 10 p.m., when an Army soldier announced our names for departure. Everyone was thrilled, including me. "Wow! Thank you, God, for such good news." I didn't know whether or not my name was on the list, but when the soldier announced four names, mine was not among them. It was good that my friends were moving on but disappointing that I was not among them. Sometimes it is easy to think you have bad luck and start complaining to God. That is how I felt at that moment.

At the same time, I had a mindset that if anything happened beyond my capability or control, it was for my good. I told myself maybe there was another great opportunity waiting for me. When my sisters-, brother- and mother-in-law were leaving, everyone was sad as I was not with them on this journey. We had such an abnormal condition. We couldn't celebrate the happiness of their moving from the base because I was not with them. I was running here and there, talking with IOM, the Army, and IRC, trying to find out why we were being separated. It was not enough that we had already parted from our families in Afghanistan; now, the same thing was happening here. I did what I could, but nothing changed. The IOM promised to send me to Florida within a few days. A month later, I again emailed Sima Quraishi, the Muslim Women Resource Center executive director, and explained the situation. She told me if I would like to come to Chicago, she would share my information with Refugee One and ask them to take my case. I told her to please proceed. I needed to leave as soon as possible.

Meanwhile, my sister-in-law was trying to get the Lutheran Resettlement Agency to take my case. Refugee One picked my case first and sent me the departure date about a month later, on January 14. Still, it was a long time to wait. I was trying to negotiate a closing date, but Refugee One Agency told me the date was already set, and IOM had agreed to the date. I had no other option rather than to accept the date. Since my wife's family had left, I was utterly alone. It was a bad time, but I distracted myself with movies, writing books, and social media until my departure.

33. Love, Divorce, Rape, and Other Cases at the Base

More than 15,000 people evacuated Afghans temporarily lived at this military base. There were different types of people. We had responsible people and families and those who were irresponsible. Most of the Afghan special forces and Army personnel (01,02,03, KPF, and other groups) had also been evacuated to the base. One of our Afghan translators told me how the Army had caught two couples in the forest. Fortunately, they were over 18, and the only advice the Army could give them was to stay out of the woods, where there were many animals, so as not get bitten by them.

Published on *military.com*: "Afghan Evacuees at Fort McCoy Face Charges of Domestic Violence and Sex with Minors" and "Two Afghan evacuees who live at Fort McCoy in Wisconsin have been arrested in unrelated cases. One was charged with crimes against a minor and received a 30-year sentence; the other charged with assaulting his wife received a ten-year sentence."

In addition to these problems, refugees had the same problems as everyone else. There were several divorces because many women discovered the new power they had in the U.S. Many couples weren't actually married but said they were, hoping their cases would be expedited more quickly.

Rumors and gossip flew around the base. For instance, "a famous male singer from Afghanistan had been evacuated to the U.S., leaving his wife and eight kids behind in Kabul. A hardcore drug addict, he brought his team to Fort McCoy, where he stole liquor from the PX and threw nightly parties". I witnessed how some people spread rumors that he was an outstanding and proud singer of Afghanistan.

There was even a rumor being spread about me. My wife called to say she heard I had married someone else. "Ha, ha. How funny." I joked. As her family, her mother, sisters, and brothers were with me, she knew it was fake news.

A good decision made by Fort McCoy officials was separating underage girls who had left Afghanistan alone. They sent these kids to specific hostels to join other kids and learn the language and culture.

34. 45 Days in "Prison."

On December 19, one of my roommates, Mr. Mohammad Mohammdi Husain) tested positive for COVID-19. Public Health quarantined him for two weeks and our whole building for seven days. After seven days had expired, we were tested again. Unfortunately, more than half of the building still tested positive. I and some other roommates were negative. Public Health decided to separate us. This time they sent the negative people to another building and kept the positive people together in another building.

Four people from our building went to the 1723 building on December 28. As we had been with positive people, we were quarantined for seven more days. Three of my roommates had flights between January 1 and 10. Unfortunately, their flights were canceled because they were still in quarantine.

My flight was on January 14, the date that I would be out of quarantine. On January 5, the Public Health Department tested us again; unfortunately, one of our neighbors, Paiman, who was with his wife, tested positive. This was more than we could imagine. Public Health asked them to leave the building and directed them to another building. they said, "We are not leaving this building unless we can return to our first building." The situation grew worse. When my friend and I asked Public Health to resettle us in another building, they said they didn't have enough space. "We have just one building for those who test positive and another for those testing negative." Finally, they decided to move those of us who had tested negative downstairs and those testing positive upstairs. We were expecting the test on January 12, but unfortunately, the Public Health personnel didn't appear. My flight was canceled again.

On January 16, they tested us again, and we learned of a new rule issued just two days earlier. We were to stay in quarantine for twenty-five days even if we tested negative. I asked for an explanation and they said it was because I had been in the same building with those who had tested positive. "Then why didn't you separate us? "I asked but never got a reply. As we were all depressed, our negotiations didn't go well. We were promised our flight would be rescheduled for next year between January 28 and February 3, 2022. Hearing this calmed us down somewhat until they put us in a building where we were confined twenty-four hours a day to our beds except to use the toilets. It felt like being in prison. Fortunately, I had limited use of the internet on my phone. Although I had bought an unlimited package, the T-Mobile sim cards were not applicable to my Indian module.

Meanwhile, I was writing a book titled *Be Your Own Boss*. I had already downloaded the reference books, so I was able to use my time to complete the first draft. While running the business campaign, I was also giving hope to Afghans, so they could bear the situation and start building our country. My followers increased from 52k to 68k, which was another excellent achievement.

I had online interviews with different national and international media and more with Voice of America – Ashna Radio. I didn't tell my Facebook followers that I was in one of the camps in the U.S. If I had told them, it would have had a negative impact. First, they would not have believed my campaigns, and second, the level of hopelessness might discourage the young generation who had been left behind in Afghanistan. Though many people asked about my location, I preferred not to answer. I also asked my mother and family in Afghanistan not to reveal my location to anyone. If someone asked, they were to say that I was in India pursuing my Ph.D.

The forty-five days in quarantine were not as bad as I had anticipated. I enjoyed communicating with my fans on social media, listening to music, and writing books. Finally, on January 26, 2022, Public Health knocked on our door and tested us again. Everyone was negative, and we were sent back to our first building, 2517. On the 27th, the Public Health staff revisited us and told us that our flight would be between January 28 and February 3, 2022. The only exception was Siam Pasarly, whose flight would be on February 6, 2022.

It was not good news, and I didn't believe it. I went to IRC (International Rescue Committee) on Jan. 28 to check my status. They confirmed the February 6 date. I was sitting at my desk on February 6 alone. No one had come to tell me the date or time of my flight. I tried to be happy for the people who came to say goodbye. They respected me, and I wished all of them good luck. Still, it was disappointing to know that everyone was leaving while I was not. When that lucky day of my departure finally occurred, I would also be happy.

35. No Way to Pursue My Ph.D.

From the beginning, we had one common problem: limited Wi-Fi and poor internet speed. Every day we walked to different areas to find a strong Wi-Fi signal so we could contact our family members, check our social media, and download some books. Many people preferred to download movies as that was their favorite choice of entertainment.

I found it more stimulating to write business articles such as *"Digital Revolution and Entrepreneurship"* and publish them in India as a marketing ecosystem book. Later, I changed my research topic to *Refugee Entrepreneurship,* which focused on the recent evacuation of Afghans to the USA. Because of the time difference, I also conducted meetings after midnight between 2 and 3 a.m., during all kinds of weather and strong wind. I had been a top scholar at the university. At the military camp, I lacked the resources for research and the dedication I once had to be well-prepared for meetings or classes and develop course guidelines and exams. Still, I forced myself to handle the situation. Finally, after discussing it with my supervisor, I wrote an e-mail explaining my country's condition, life in the camp, the lack of facilities, and other problems. I requested a postponement of my Ph.D. until April 2022. I had to do this because I lacked the resources and the ability to pay my fees. It was a great solution at the time. In the meantime, my classmates from India were texting me to ask why I was not coming to the university. My desk and office were still vacant and available until I officially relinquished them to another scholar.

36. Lack of Management Doesn't Mean We Have Bad Luck

It was February 7, 2022, at 12:43 a.m., when I was supposed to be in the waiting room for my departure to Chicago. Instead, I was the only person remaining in the entire building because of mismanagement and lack of communication between IRC and IOM. Needless to say, the situation made me tense. Earlier, at 10 a.m., an Army soldier had explained the miscommunication between IOM and IRC regarding my case. He was sympathetic to my situation and encouraged me to stay strong as my departure would be in just a few more days.

To be honest, I couldn't help but think, "Why me?"

I couldn't sleep because that question kept running through my head. Why was I the last person to evacuate the base? Had I been singled out to complete the mission? Was there a special opportunity that only I was qualified to finish? Such are the fantasies that ran through my head while I waited to fall asleep.

Meanwhile, my wife called and asked if everything was all right. I told her the story of my departure delay, and she was also upset. Then she told me some distressing news. Our soon-to-be-born son was not moving as he should have, and she was not feeling well. She had scheduled an appointment with her medical doctor for a checkup. My sister-in-law called, assuming that I was already in Chicago. I told her I wished I was in Chicago but still at Fort McCoy military base. When she heard that, she felt very bad for me.

I wrote a lot to pass the time, then grew tired of writing. I tried to sleep, but tension kept me from falling asleep. To distract myself, I started writing articles on business development for the Afghans who left Afghanistan and then uploaded them on Facebook. I still couldn't sleep. To distract myself, I watched an Indian movie, but after two hours, I was still tossing and turning in my bed as I tried and failed to fall asleep. I couldn't help but be angry with IOM and IRC. Although they had supported us well enough in most instances, they had some unqualified people managing our travel arrangements. Because of their deficiencies, I was alone in the base cooling my heels for several more days. I was the last civilian to leave.

37. Emergency Conditions: "I Need to Get to Pakistan!"

On February 7, 2022, I woke up, checked my WhatsApp, and saw my wife's message. She was in her eighth month of pregnancy and not in good condition. "All day, I have been running here and there in the hospital," she wrote. "The baby is not moving the way it should. The doctors are recommending an operation, but I don't want to have it." That was alarming news. I tried to call her, but her phone was off. I called friends and relatives to ask if they could offer her their support. As her phone was not working, no one could reach her.

After calling many times without an answer, I decided to leave for Pakistan. It was morning, the weather was cold and everything was covered with snow. Going to the local Army office, I knocked on the door and requested we talk.

I shared my situation and asked for their help. First, they told me to calm down and then advised me to reconsider going to Pakistan. I insisted that I needed to go and implored them to help me find a way. Seeing my desperation, they gave me the address of the International Organization for Migration (IOM) and said this organization would find a way for me to leave.

Though the weather was very cold and I wore jackets and scarves, walking on the snow almost for one mile was difficult. I was hungry and the restaurant closed at 9:00 am, so I went to eat and then went to the IOM. I met one tall, energetic and happy man; he started speaking Dari by asking, "How are you?" (Chetor hasti), I replied, "Well I don't feel happy." He asked why and I explained. He said, "See I am an Afghan interpreter here and I also had a similar case. He explained the pros and cons and then advised me if I have money I should go, but I would need a Pakistan visa. Unfortunately, mine had expired.

Going to Pakistan required a ticket, visa, and other expenses and I had no money to cover the costs. I tried to collect the necessary information on how to get to Pakistan. I went to IOM and explained my situation to a responsible woman who told me I would be resettled within a week. "We understand your dilemma, but now is not a good time for you to leave. Please don't jeopardize your life." I returned to my room and prayed to Allah to help me solve this problem. Later, some of my friends at the base came by and persuaded me not to do anything impulsive. It was then 8:45 am, and I was still waiting to hear from my wife.

I waited all day and into the night. I asked my relatives to visit the hospital and tell me what my wife had decided about the operation. Finally, my relatives located my wife at the hospital and discovered her phone had not been charged. She was in bed waiting to deliver our child. My daughter is very clever. I was able to talk with her on the phone. "Don't worry, Baba. I am with my Mom. I am praying for her to have a safe delivery," my daughter said.

38. "Forget It! Peace in Afghanistan is Impossible!"

Every night at 7:00 p.m., we would gather for dinner and discuss such issues as religion and race from different perspectives. That evening, the topics were Afghanistan and the Taliban. We talked about our former government and whether or not it was possible to have reconstruction and remain a peaceful country.

Some people thought we should forget about these issues and start new lives. Others said they had never planned to return to Afghanistan. It made me sad to hear they thought there was no future in their birth country, our land, and the Afghan people. On one level, they were right, but their negativity, hating their birth country, the land, and the people, was not easy for me to accept. Even on the base, I couldn't stop thinking about Afghanistan, both the good and bad times.

Afghanistan has had many problems, but it is still my country. How can I abandon my country to others? I was negotiating with the whole group as a one-man army to explain that if we don't think, work and change our country, then who will do it? Some Afghans said they are not responsible for building Afghanistan; they want to enjoy their lives in a peaceful world. They were right to do that. We still have many other people eager to go back and work for their country and its people.

In the meantime, I was posting my daily entries on Facebook and other social media websites. I attracted huge numbers of people. I was very positive in my postings about business ideas and other opportunities on social media. I welcomed readers, most of them younger and former government officials. They sent messages asking to meet with me to discuss these opportunities further. Some requested regular Zoom meetings to develop action plans for my ideas. I was also getting positive responses from Facebook fans. It was rewarding to see younger people eagerly follow my page.

One of my Facebook followers sent me a screenshot where he put my picture on his phone screen and told me that we learned a lot from your Facebook and YouTube channel. He also said we have downloaded your videos and distributed them among students at the universities, schools, and communities. It was a great moment for me. With such positive feedback, I promised to continue the effort and make more videos.

Meanwhile, (while writing the above paragraph) I got a message from the Deputy of the National Environmental Protection Agency in Afghanistan. After complimenting me on my efforts, he asked my advice on how to start his own business. He was a qualified lecturer, and I respect him. His message prompted me to turn my attention to motivational talks, quotes, and videos. In the beginning, I thought these activities might be useless, but I changed my mind when I got good feedback and positive comments. On the other hand, I knew of people at the base who had little to do and became depressed and suicidal. I did not have that problem because I had found ways to be occupied: working, writing, and using social media. I responded to messages, shared my feedback, and advised others on how to develop a business plan.

I believe in individual growth. If we grow as individuals, we will positively impact society. Just as individuals can improve and grow, Afghanistan can be rebuilt into a strong, independent country once again.

39. My Wife's Operation in Pakistan

I can fight with the whole world and make the impossible possible, but only when I am at peace with my wife. She is the source of my power and strength and my weakness. On February 7, 2022, my wife was admitted to the hospital in Peshawar when she was eight months pregnant. The hospital doctors said a normal delivery would not be safe, and she would need a surgical delivery called a cesarean section. Until then, she would have to stay in bed. That was worrisome news. I didn't fall asleep until 2:00 a.m.

Inside the base, I had limited internet and phone access. WhatsApp didn't work. My wife needed to speak to me so I could help her with her decision. She tried to reach me but couldn't. She called her sister

Raihana who was already in the US. Then she called someone at Fort McCoy. That's when the soldiers informed me about her condition. I quickly turned on my laptop's hotspot. Normally Wi-Fi didn't work in the building, but I was using the Wi-Fi accelerator via my laptop. When I got it set up and opened on WhatsApp, I received a flood of messages from my wife, all my sisters-in-law, my mother, my brother, and some friends. I quickly called my wife and found her in tears because she thought I had forgotten her. That night I slept only five hours. When I talked to my wife again, I admitted that I felt guilty that I had not been able to speak with her when she needed me, although it was actually because of a faulty connection with our phones. When I finally reached her, I asked her to bring me up to date on what was happening. She said she had accepted the doctor's recommendation for an operation but needed blood. "Don't worry, "I said. "I will handle it." I kept calling my friends and network in Pakistan for blood donations. Meanwhile, the doctor told her they had solved the blood problem.

I knew my wife would be afraid of an operation, especially because she was alone without my family or me to support her. Although I could understand and sympathize with her situation from afar, she needed my presence now more than at any other time. I was in touch with her by phone and learned her operation would be the day after next, which meant she would be in the hospital for at least two more days. Our daughter Malala, who is five years old, said, "Don't worry, Baba, I am with Mama."

It was so touching to hear this from her. At the same time, I was concerned about my daughter's well-being and how long it would be advisable for her to stay at the hospital. So, my wife sent Malala to her teacher's house. My father and other family members had yet to hear that my wife was in Peshawar. I purposely didn't tell them. I knew my father might be offended that I had not shared my wife's situation, but I did this out of security concerns. I could just hear him saying, "You mean you don't trust your own family?" All these questions were running through my head. Ultimately, I decided to share the information as my father might know someone in Peshawar who could help my wife.

40. God's Gift to Me

On Wednesday, February 9, 2022, at 12:40 am, the Army came to my building with my final briefing for Chicago. It was good news. On the same day, my wife had her operation. After a difficult time, she delivered a baby boy. My relatives sent me a picture of our son. Although my wife had delivered a healthy baby, she had tested positive for Covid, and the doctor put her in a separate room. Though I was very happy about my son, I was sad that there was no family member to support my wife. My entire family was in Afghanistan, and I was in the US. She needed my help.

Although I had my final IOM departure briefing in the morning, I could not sleep that night. At 7:00 a.m., an Army soldier told me to be at the Red Cross office, where I would join other team members for an IOM meeting. I followed his directions, although I had no internet connection and had to use Wi-Fi instead.

Meanwhile, I was in contact with my wife at the hospital. Since I had limited internet access, I got a hotspot from another guest on the base. I learned that my wife's and son's situation was not good. My wife told me to call my friends and ask them to come with their wives or mother to support her. Thus, I began calling friends to ask them to send their family members to help my wife. First, I called Mr. Baz Mohammad Abid, a journalist and social activist who had left Peshawar for Kabul.

Then I called Mr. Baz Muhammad Afsarzai, my best business friend, to send his family, but he was in Kabul. I called Mr. Imran Saidy, my best friend whose wife used to be in Peshawar; unfortunately, they were also in Kabul, but he gave me the phone number of one of his friends, Gul Roze, and his wife, who might visit my family. I also contacted Mr. Aftab, a lecturer at Rana University in Kabul. We used to meet and discuss business issues. He was in Islamabad but promised to send his family to the hospital in the morning. My uncle, Mr. Ghousdden Boura, called to congratulate me. I talked for a few seconds, and he said he would get back to me.

My wife's condition was not good, so she was not in a good frame of mind. I called my father and described the situation: "My wife and kid are not feeling well. Please pray." My father, mother, brothers, and sisters prayed and recited the holy Quran for my wife and kid. Meanwhile, I attended an IOM meeting, although I paid little attention to what they talked about. My whole focus was on Peshawar and my wife. While I was trying to reach her, I lost the connection. In the meantime, I learned that my friend Gul Roze was on his way to the hospital.

Finally, Gul Roze's wife could stay with my wife for a day but then had to leave. Late that evening, the hospital released my wife and sent her home. Because of her operation, she couldn't feed the baby or prepare food for herself. When I got her phone call, she was in tears. "We are losing the baby, and I am in poor condition. Please do something." I tried calling my friends in Peshawar to see if anyone could support her. By then, it was 10:00 p.m., and everyone I asked said they would visit her the next day. They didn't understand the seriousness of the situation.

Finally, my brother-in-law, Mr. Jabar Nazari, said that he knew of a family who could support my wife. They went to our home at 11:00 in the evening. I will be ever grateful to this family; they saved my wife and our child. Unfortunately, they couldn't stay any longer; after they left, my wife's condition worsened. I tried to call and ask the family to come back, but their WhatsApp was off. After a few minutes, my wife called to say the baby was asleep, and she seemed to be more relaxed. I asked her to handle the pressure for just one more night, and then I would handle the situation.

The next day I arranged for two women to look after my wife day and night. I called my friends and the Afghanistan Embassy in Pakistan to find qualified women for long-term care. Early the following day, I called Mr. Haji Ali Ahmad, who had been referred to us by my brother-in-law. I explained our situation and asked him to find qualified women to care for my wife and son. He said, "Why don't you send your family to my home? My wife, daughter, niece, and sisters will assist her. We have a big sunny yard that will be good for your wife." I accepted the invitation on the spot with one condition: I would pay all expenses, but he declined my offer. I was finally relieved to have a place for my family to go. Meanwhile, I started preparations to leave the base for Chicago.

On February 10, 2022, at 11:00 a.m., an Army soldier came and told me to be at the CP (Command Post) for departure. We waited at the 2409 block for a final briefing and were told to be ready to leave at 2:00 am. At 9:00 pm, during the IRC briefing, an Army soldier called out: "Who is Pasarly?" I responded and was told to hurry up and let's go to the Command Post, where I faced two gentlemen: one from the FBI and the other from DHS (Department of Homeland Security).

41. The FBI and the DHS

On February 10, 2022, at 9:05 pm., I faced two agents, one from the Federal Bureau of Investigation (FBI) and the other from the Department of Homeland Services (DHS) who had asked a translator to accompany us. Although I could speak English, they insisted on having a translator present. We rode in their car. It was the first time to meet people from the FBI and DHS. Of course, I was tense; I didn't know what was happening. On the way, I asked them to tell me where we were going. They said they would explain when we got to the office. One of them volunteered, "No worries. We just have a couple of questions to ask." I said, "OK," as if I had a choice.

When we arrived at their office, I was taken to a meeting room with a camera and two other FBI agents. Before starting, they introduced themselves and showed me their ID cards. I introduced myself, "How may I help you?" The questions and length of the meeting must remain confidential, but it was not a bad meeting. They thanked me and accompanied me back to my barracks. Besides my concern for my family, this episode only added to my anxiety. At the barracks, I slept until 2:00 am, then left for IOM. I traveled to Chicago by car and arrived at 9:00 am. An hour later, I met my case worker Mr. Kefayatullah Walizai. He took me to the Refugee One Resettlement Agency. After meeting with this organization, I got my documents, completed my paperwork, and went to my apartment. I finally had a home again.

42. Conclusion

Leaving your country is not easy. Leaving Afghanistan was the most difficult and unwelcome decision of my life. I have visited many countries, but I never, ever intended to leave Afghanistan or invest my money in any other country. I even had a chance to live and work in Italy. But I chose to go back to Afghanistan not because I still have accounts in Afghan banks and not because my companies are registered there, but because I love Afghanistan.

Although this is my story, it is not only my story. There were thousands of people who wanted to escape and save their lives. They left their homes, families, and children to survive and escape the violence.

I know many of these people. After more than a year, they are struggling to reunify with their families. This has been a horrible time in history for Afghanistan and its people. I hope peace and civility can return to Afghanistan, and we who want to can also return to serve the country we love. We are refugees, not terrorists, but we are victims of terrorists.

It has been the purpose of this book to show the realities of what we endured to escape. And we are the fortunate ones who have escaped. Many have been left behind or have been killed. But we are also unfortunate because we have had to leave the country, family, and friends we love and have lived with all our lives.

I'm not sure whom to blame for the fall of Afghanistan - the Taliban, the government, or the international community - but the people of Afghanistan are paying the price.

It is important to mention that Fort McCoy, a beautiful, clean, well-equipped military area, was turned into the Afghan Refugees Village. We thank all the soldiers, workers, cleaners, and officials at Fort McCoy for their tireless support.

To conclude, my love for Afghanistan and my people increased with time. I love my country, and I'll be back when I can take an active role in the development of Afghanistan. I am neither a military nor a political person. I am convinced that to implement my vision for Afghanistan, we must have a stable, reliable, and comprehensive government. If the situation changes and it is safe to return to my country, I will go back and begin implementing my plans.

Made in United States
Orlando, FL
25 February 2024